THE FACTS ON THE MASONIC LODGE

JOHN ANKERBERG & JOHN WELDON

HARVEST HOUSE™ PUBLISHERS

EUGENE, OREGON

Cover by Terry Dugan Design, Minneapolis, Minnesota

THE FACTS ON SERIES
John Ankerberg and John Weldon

The Facts on Angels
The Facts on Creation vs. Evolution
The Facts on Halloween
The Facts on Homosexuality
The Facts on Islam
The Facts on Jehovah's Witnesses
The Facts on the King James Only Debate
The Facts on the Masonic Lodge
The Facts on the Mormon Church
The Facts on the New Age Movement
The Facts on the Occult
The Facts on Roman Catholicism

THE FACTS ON THE MASONIC LODGE
Copyright © 1989 by The Ankerberg Theological Research Institute
Published by Harvest House Publishers
Eugene, Oregon 97402

Ankerberg, John, 1945–
   The facts on the Masonic Lodge / John Ankerberg and John Weldon.
      p. cm. — (Facts on series)
Includes bibliographical references.
   ISBN 0-7369-1113-8 (pbk.)
   1. Freemasonry—Religious aspects—Christianity. 2. Freemasonry—United States. I. Weldon, John. II. Title.
   HS495 .A55 2003
   366'.1—dc21
                                                            2002010764

Printed in the United States of America

   03   04   05   06   07   08   / VP-CF/   9   8   7   6   5   4   3   2   1

Contents

Section III
Where Does the Masonic Ritual
Conflict with the Bible?

About This Book

Is the Masonic Lodge compatible with Christianity? The Lodge challenged "The John Ankerberg Show's" teachings on Masonry. They claimed Masonry was not a religion and did not in any way conflict with Christianity. But is this true?

A Masonic guest on our television program told us that the Ritual was the authoritative source for all Masons—and he was correct. In this book, we have cited Masonic Ritual and shown how it conflicts with Christian teaching.

We also wrote to all 50 of the Grand Lodges in the United States and asked them which Masonic authors and books they would recommend as the most authoritative commentaries concerning the teachings of Masonry. We will report to you what they said. Then we will compare the commentary of their recommended authors with some of the teachings of biblical Christianity to answer the question, "Is Christianity compatible with the teachings of the Masonic Lodge?"

The information we present is fully documented from authoritative Masonic sources and is confirmed as accurate by Masons and former Masons.

In this book, we have stressed the Ritual of the Blue Lodge—the first three degrees of Masonry (Entered Apprentice, Fellow Craft, and Master Mason)—since these are the degrees through which *every* Mason must pass.*

---

* In *The Secret Teachings of the Masonic Lodge: A Christian Appraisal* (Moody Press, 1990), we cover many important additional facts and issues in Masonry that space does not permit us to address here. We cover not only the Blue Lodge, but also the York and Scottish Rites. Together, these combine 40 additional degrees of Masonry (10 in the York Rite and 30 in the Scottish Rite) that a Mason may complete. However, most Masons complete only the Blue Lodge, and this is why we have concentrated upon it here.

For those needing information on the following subjects, we suggest they consult our book. The issues we discuss include: the worldwide influence and global goals of Masonry, how Masonry is influencing the church, a specific analysis of the theology of Masonry on the topics of God, Jesus Christ, salvation, life after death, and its views on the Bible. In addition, we show how Masonry is related to the ancient mystery religions; what characteristics it has in common with cultism; how Masonry encourages occult involvement; and many other important issues.

We have examined the standard interpretations of the Blue Lodge rituals given by Masons. Most Masons believe that Blue Lodge Masonry makes one as full or complete a Mason as one can (or needs) to be. But an important fact must be noted. While the Blue Lodge is Masonry, and while it is the Masonry of most Masons, it is not all that Masonry constitutes. Some Masons would view Blue Lodge Masonry as it is usually interpreted, as an initial or beginning form of Masonry, and maintain that the real substance of Masonry—its lifeblood—lies in the higher degrees and in the initiate's search for their true meaning. Some Masons would even consider Blue Lodge Masonry as only the *cover* of the book, but not the book itself. These Masons would say that to truly understand Masonry one must open the book and read what lies *within* the cover. What one finds there will shock even many Masons. (For details consult our book and e.g., 16/12.)*

As Sovereign Grand Commander Henry C. Claussen admitted, "It must be apparent that the Blue Lodge...degrees cannot explain the whole of Masonry. They are the foundation....An initiate may imagine he understands the ethics, symbols and enigmas, whereas a true explanation of these is reserved for the more adept" (94:148).

It is our sincere hope that this book will encourage Christian Masons to look seriously and frankly at Masonry and ask themselves: Can a Christian who follows Jesus Christ and accepts biblical authority really be a Mason? In good conscience, can he justify his involvement in Masonry?

As one Anglican vicar, also a Mason observed, "I for one can never understand how anyone who takes an exclusive view of Christ as the only complete revelation of God's truth can become a Freemason without suffering from spiritual schizophrenia" (12:234).

---

* Reference information throughout this book is found in parentheses and includes the bibliography number found in the back of this book and the reference page number in the work cited. Where a book has more than one volume, the volume is identified with a Roman numeral.

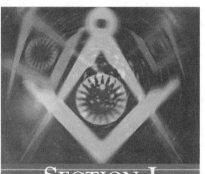

SECTION I

Introduction to Masonry

1

What is Masonry?

As a fraternity, we are always ready to be judged—
severely and critically (101:1).

FRANCIS G. PAUL,
33rd Degree Sovereign Grand Commander
(*The Northern Light*, May 1988)

Masonry (also known as Freemasonry or "the Lodge") is a powerful, centuries-old fraternal order that, according to Masonic authorities, began in the early eighteenth century. According to most Masonic authorities, modern Masonry (also called "speculative" Masonry) can be traced to the founding of the first Grand Lodge in London in A.D. 1717 (70,I:131, 152; 1:3; 15:12).

The Lodge is also a secret society. To maintain its secrets, Masonry uses symbolism, secret oaths, and secret rituals to instruct new members, called "initiates." Each new member swears during these secret ceremonies to remain loyal to the Lodge and its teachings. The teachings instruct each new candidate how he is to serve and the rewards he can expect.

Let us examine the definition of Masonry as given by Masons themselves. In Albert G. Mackey's *Revised Encyclopedia of Freemasonry* he states, "All [Masons] unite in declaring it to be a system of morality, by the practice of which its members may advance their spiritual interest, and mount by the theological ladder from the Lodge on earth to the Lodge in heaven" (96,I:269).

Other respected Masonic authorities define Masonry in the following words:

> "It is a science which is engaged in the search after Divine Truth, and which employs symbolism as its method of instruction" (96,I:269).

> "[Masonry is] that religious and mystical society whose aim is moral perfection on the basis of general equality and fraternity" (96,I:269).

> "Freemasonry, in its broadest and most comprehensive sense, is a system of morality and social ethics, a primitive religion, and a philosophy of life...incorporating a broad humanitarianism....It is a religion without a creed, being of no sect but finding truth in all....It seeks truth but does not define truth..." (36:234).

A man who becomes a Mason is defined by Masonic authorities as being "one who has been initiated into the mysteries of the fraternity of Freemasonry" (96,I:378).

What we present in this book is an analysis of *Masonry itself*, as stated by Masonic authorities recommended to us by at least half of the Grand Lodges in the United States (see Question 2). The Grand Lodge of each state sets the Ritual and the interpretation of that Ritual which is to be followed by the members of that state.

2

What is the final authority for the teachings presented in each Masonic Lodge?

If anyone is going to investigate the teachings of the Masonic Lodge, who or what is the authority that they should listen to?

When we asked this question on our television program to Mr. Bill Mankin, a thirty-second degree Mason, he said, "The authoritative source for Masonry is the ritual. The ritual—what happens in the Lodge, what goes on" (1:3,5).

When one examines Masonry *today* and compares the different manuals containing the ritual for each state, it is apparent that *today* the ritual and the interpretations given are almost identical. Therefore, the Ritual in the Masonic manuals can be considered the authoritative teachings of the Lodge. As former Worshipful Master Jack Harris reveals: "In

[all] other states…the principle and the doctrines [of the Ritual] are exactly the same. The wording only varies slightly" (13:29).

But we wanted to know which authors and books Masons themselves recommend to outsiders as authoritative. In order to answer this question, a letter was sent to each of the 50 Grand Lodges in America. We addressed the letter to the Grand Master of each of the Grand Lodges and asked him to respond to the following question: "As an official Masonic leader, which books and authors do you recommend as being authoritative on the subject of Freemasonry?"

Half of all the Grand Lodges in the United States responded, that is, 25 of the 50 (AZ, CO, CT, DC, DE, IA, ID, IL, IN, KS, LA, MA, ME, MI, MO, NJ, NM, NY, OH, PA, SC, TX, UT, VA, WI). Remember: For each state there is no higher authority than its Grand Lodge.

3

Which books and authors have been recommended by the Grand Lodges as being authoritative for Masons?

When we received a reply from a Grand Lodge, we compared which authors and books they recommended as being authoritative for them with the replies from the other Grand Lodges. These are the authors that the Grand Lodges recommended:

> 44%—of the Grand Lodges recommended *Coil's Masonic Encyclopedia* by Henry Wilson Coil.
>
> 36%—*The Builders* by Joseph Fort Newton
>
> 32%—*Mackey's Revised Encyclopedia of Freemasonry* by Albert G. Mackey
>
> 24%—*Introduction to Freemasonry* by Carl H. Claudy
>
> 24%—*The Newly-Made Mason* by H. L. Haywood

20%—*A Masonic Reader's Guide* by Alphonse Cerza

20%—*History of Freemasonry* by Robert F. Gould

20%—*The Craft and Its Symbols* by Allen E. Roberts

16%—*Morals and Dogma* by Albert Pike

Notice that the Grand Lodges, by their responses, reveal that Coil, Newton, and Mackey are the three leading Masonic authorities (cf. 49:172; 57:8; 51,I:130; 57:148).

Because of the high esteem in which these authors are held by the Grand Lodges, we will often document our analysis of Masonry from their texts. At the same time, we have not neglected the other Masonic authors recommended by the Grand Lodges. We have tried to quote fairly from them all.

We have done all of this so that Masons cannot say that we have based our arguments on material that no Mason would consider authoritative and reliable. Masons must acknowledge that these authors and books do represent their most authoritative interpreters of Freemasonry.

4

What are the Blue Lodge, the Scottish Rite, and the York Rite?

All men who become Masons go through the first three degrees of the Blue Lodge. The Blue Lodge is the parent or mother Lodge of Freemasonry. In the Blue Lodge are conferred the first three degrees: 1) the Entered Apprentice, where a man is initiated into the beginning mysteries of the fraternity of Freemasonry; 2) the degree of Fellow Craft; and 3) the Master Mason degree.

After passing these three degrees in the Blue Lodge, the candidate may choose not to proceed further at all, or he may choose to proceed higher along one or both of two branches in Masonry.

One branch is known as the Scottish Rite, which advances by numerical degrees, beginning with the fourth and ending with the thirty-second, the thirty-third degree being either active or honorary. The other major branch is the York Rite, which goes through what is called the "Chapter," "Council," and "Commandery" degrees, ending with the degree of Knights Templar.

If a Mason is suspended or expelled from his Blue Lodge, it automatically severs his connection from all other Masonic bodies. Anyone who passes the first three degrees and becomes a Master Mason may visit Blue Lodges other than his own.

On the next page we present a diagram of the three Blue Lodge degrees that every Mason must take, plus the optional degrees of the York and Scottish Rites (74, cf. 100. Note: Only the Scottish Rite cites its degrees by number—the York Rite designates its degrees by name. For example, the fourth degree of the York Rite is termed "Mark Master" whereas in the Scottish Rite the degree is simply called the fourth degree.):

Blue Lodge Degrees and Optional York and Scottish Rites

Blue Lodge

1. Entered Apprentice
2. Fellow Craft
3. Master Mason

York Rite	*Scottish Rite*
Chapter (capitular degrees)	*Lodge of Perfection*
Mark Master	4. Secret Master
	5. Perfect Master
	6. Intimate Secretary
Past Master (Virtual)	7. Provost & Judge
	8. Intendant of the Building
	9. Elu of the Nine
	10. Elu of the Fifteen
Most Excellent Master	11. Elu of the Twelve
	12. Master Architect
	13. Royal Arch of Solomon
Royal Arch Mason	14. Perfect Elu
Council (cryptic degrees)	*Chapter Rose Croix*
	15. Knight of the East or Sword
	16. Prince of Jerusalem
Royal Master	17. Knight of the East & West
	18. Knight Rose Croix
	Council of Kadosh
	19. Grand Pontiff
Select Master	20. Master of the Symbolic Lodge
	21. Noachite or Prussian Knight
	22. Knight of the Royal Axe
Super Excellent Master	23. Chief of the Tabernacle
	24. Prince of the Tabernacle
Commandery (chivalric degrees)	25. Knight of the Brazen Serpent
Order of the Red Cross	26. Prince of Mercy
	27. Knight Commander of the Temple
	28. Knight of the Sun
Order of the Knights of Malta	29. Knight of St. Andrew
	30. Knight Kadosh
	Consistory
	31. Inspector Inquisitor
Order of Knights Templar Commandery	32. Master of the Royal Secret
	33. (Active or Honorary)

SECTION II

Is Freemasonry a Religion?

5

Is Freemasonry another religion?

There are approximately two million Masons in the United States. Many Masons are Christians and many are from other religious faiths. The question is, "Are those members of the Masonic Lodge willingly or unwillingly participating in another religion—the religion of Freemasonry?"

Most Masons are adamant in stating that Freemasonry is not a religion. Alphonse Cerza, former Grand Historian of the Grand Lodge of Illinois, and many of the Masons who have written to us argued that Freemasonry is not a religion because of the following: 1) It does not meet the definition of a religion; 2) it offers no system or teaching of salvation; 3) it has no creed, no confession of faith, no theology, and no ritual of worship; and 4) it has no symbols that are religious, like the symbols that are found in a church (1:2, cf. 73:41).

To quote Bill Mankin: "All we are saying is that if you as an individual adopt the principles represented [in Freemasonry]...that you will be a better person. Not that you are going to go to heaven" (1:2).

Is Freemasonry a religion? Masonic author Alphonse Cerza in his book *Let There Be Light—A Study in Anti-Masonry* quoted Dr. M. W. Thomas S. Roy, Grand Master of the Grand Lodge in Massachusetts, in his address to that Lodge. Dr. Roy stated: "By any definition of religion accepted by our critics, we cannot qualify as a religion..." (73:41).

To see if Cerza and Roy are correct, let us begin with the definition of religion from *Webster's New World Dictionary* which defines religion as: "1) [a] belief in a divine or superhuman power...to be obeyed and worshipped as the Creator and ruler of the universe; 2) expression of...[this] belief in conduct and ritual" (106).

Now, would any Mason deny that Freemasonry fits this definition of religion as given by Webster? Is it not true that Masonry demands belief in a Supreme

Being? Would any Mason deny that their authoritative Ritual describes exactly how they are to express this belief in conduct and ceremony? In brief, can any Freemason say Masonry is not a religion? The answer is obviously "No."

But Masons do not need to take our word for it. They only need to listen to their respected Masonic authorities. The number-one author recommended by the Grand Lodges was Henry Wilson Coil and his *Masonic Encyclopedia*. Coil quotes the definition of religion given by *Funk and Wagnalls' New Standard Dictionary* (1941), and then asserts that Freemasonry fits not only this definition, but also fits the dictionary definition of what constitutes a "church." Coil states:

> "Freemasonry certainly requires a belief in the existence of, and man's dependence upon, a Supreme Being to whom he is responsible. What can a church add to that, except to bring into one fellowship those who have like feelings?...That is exactly what the Lodge does" (95:512).

In other words, Coil is saying that not only is Freemasonry a religion, but Freemasonry also functions as a religion as much as a church does.

Albert Mackey in *Mackey's Revised Encyclopedia of Freemasonry*, the third most recommended author by the Grand Lodges, quotes *Webster's* definition of religion and then comments, "Freemasonry may rightfully claim to be called a religious institution" (96,II:847).

So is Freemasonry a religion? According to *Webster's Dictionary*, according to *Funk and Wagnalls'*, and according to leading Masonic authorities Coil and Mackey as recommended by the Grand Lodges in this country, Freemasonry *is* a religion.

6

Does the Masonic Lodge teach its own plan of salvation?

Another reason Masons give as to why Freemasonry cannot be considered a religion is because "It offers no system of salvation" (1:2). In other words, they say Freemasonry has no teachings about how a man can go to heaven. But is this true?

Every candidate who enters the Blue Lodge is told again and again during the first three degrees of Masonry that God will reward those who do good deeds.

This can be documented by examining any Masonic manual that contains the Ritual of the first three degrees. In the manual under the explanation of the symbol of the "All-Seeing Eye"—one of the symbols for God—you will find these words: The "All-Seeing Eye [God]...beholds [or "pervades" (69:83)] the inmost recesses of the human heart, and *will reward us according to our works*" (58:129, emphasis added).

What is the reward Masonry teaches man will get because of his good works? Masonry teaches that God will reward man with eternal life in the "Celestial Lodge Above." This can be documented in the *Masonic Ritual and Monitor* under the explanation concerning the lambskin, or white linen apron. There it says, "He who wears the lambskin as a badge of a Mason is thereby continually reminded of *purity of life and conduct* which is *essentially necessary to his gaining admission* into that celestial Lodge above, where the Supreme Architect of the universe presides" (58:50, emphasis added; cf. 69:88).

Now does this sound to you like Freemasonry is teaching a way of salvation? If you were to hear this taught in the Lodge, wouldn't you think that Freemasonry is saying that *you* can go to the "Celestial Lodge Above" if you live a pure and honest life? Isn't that religion?

If you're a Christian, when the Lodge teaches a man that by *his* good life and by *his* good deeds God will admit him into heaven, isn't that contrary to biblical teaching? Doesn't the Bible clearly teach that salvation is *not* by a man's work—salvation is only by God's gracious provision through Jesus Christ? Ephesians 2:8,9 (NIV) very plainly says, "For it is by grace you have been saved, through faith—and this not from yourselves, it is the gift of God—not by works, so that no one can boast."

But if you are still not persuaded that Masonry is presenting a way to heaven, you should listen to Masonic authority Henry Wilson Coil, who writes the following about one of Freemasonry's religious services. In his encyclopedia he argues:

> "Freemasonry has a *religious* service to commit the body of a deceased brother to the dust whence it came, and *to speed* the *liberated spirit back* to the Great Source of Light. Many Freemasons make this flight with *no other guarantee* of a safe landing than their belief in the religion of Freemasonry" (95:512, emphasis added).

Notice he says, *"religion* of Freemasonry." From this evidence, all must conclude that Freemasonry *is* a religion because it does offer religious instruction and promises of how a man may get to heaven. In brief, Freemasonry *is* a religion because it presents its own plan of salvation.

So we have now seen that Freemasonry fits the definition of religion as given by Webster, and we've seen that it does offer its own plan of salvation—how a man can go to heaven.

7

Does the creed of the Masonic Lodge prove that it is a religion?

Some Masons say, along with Masonic apologist Alphonse Cerza, "Freemasonry cannot be a religion because it has no creed; it has no confession of faith; it has no theology, no ritual of worship" (1:2; 73:41). Let us now examine the claim that Freemasonry cannot be a religion because it has no creed.

Webster defines "creed" as: "a statement of belief, principles, or opinions on any subject" (106). Now, according to Webster, how can any Mason really say that he has no creed? No man can become a Mason without confessing his faith in a Supreme Being. Every Mason must believe in the immortality of the soul, give honorable service to God by practicing the secret arts of Masonry, say prayers to deity, and swear oaths of secrecy in God's name. These practices prove Masons have a definite creed.

In *Coil's Masonic Encyclopedia* we find:

> "Does Freemasonry have a creed...or tenet...or dogma...to which all members must adhere? Does Freemasonry continually teach and insist upon a *creed, tenet and dogma*? Does it have meetings characterized by the practice of rites and ceremonies in, and by which, its creed, tenet and dogma are illustrated, by myth, symbols and allegories? If Freemasonry were not religion, what would have to be done to make it such? *Nothing would be necessary, or at least nothing but to add more of the same*" (95:512, emphasis added).

Coil goes on to point out that not only does Freemasonry have a creed, but that the Masonic Lodge actually functions in practice as a church. For example, he writes:

> "That brings us to the real crux of the matter. The difference between a Lodge and a church is one of degree and not of kind. Some think because it [the Lodge] is not a strong or highly formalized or highly dogmatized religion, such as the Roman Catholic Church...it can be no religion at all. But a church of friends (Quakers) exhibits even less formality and ritual than does a Masonic Lodge" (95:512).

In conclusion, Coil writes, "The fact that Freemasonry is a mild religion does not mean that it is no religion" (95:512). Every Mason should listen to Henry Wilson Coil and stop asserting that they have no creed in the Lodge. If they do have their own creed, they should also admit as Coil does that they are practicing religion.

8

Does the Masonic Lodge have its own distinct doctrinal statement like a church does?

Another reason Masons give for claiming Freemasonry is not a religion is because "we have no confession of faith in a doctrinal statement such as a church does." But is this true?

How can any Mason honestly say he has no confession of faith when he *must* believe in the teachings of the Landmarks concerning the universal Fatherhood of God and brotherhood of man, when he *must* believe in immortality of the soul, when he *must* believe in a Supreme Being, and when he *must* believe that as a good Mason he will reside in the "Celestial Lodge Above" for all eternity?

Not only do Masons have a confession of faith in their own doctrinal beliefs, but their Masonic beliefs are distinctive. It can be seen that Masonry teaches *specific* religious doctrines which are not accepted by many other religions. This means Masonry's claim of not having distinctive religious doctrines is false.

This can easily be seen from Masonry's religious teaching concerning the immortality of the soul. Just ask yourself, "Do all religions believe in the doctrine of the immortality of the soul like Masons do?" The answer is "No." Seventh-Day Adventists, Jehovah's Witnesses, Armstrongites, and Buddhists, to name just a few, do not believe in the immortality of the soul as Masons do.

Do all religious people believe in a single Supreme Being as the Masons do? No. Hindus believe in millions of gods; so do Mormons. Many Buddhists do not believe in God at all.

At death, do all religious people believe as Masons do that they will reside in the "Celestial Lodge in the Sky" for all eternity? A quick examination of other people's beliefs reveals that Hindus and Buddhists believe in the extinction of the person. Mormons believe that they can become gods themselves. Jehovah's Witnesses believe that only 144,000 will get to reside in heaven and all the rest who aren't annihilated will stay on planet Earth.

In conclusion, it is absolutely clear that the Masonic Lodge does have its own distinct religious doctrinal statement just like any other religion does. That's why Masonry must be considered to be teaching religion.

9

Can any Mason honestly claim that the Lodge has no theology of its own?

Another reason Masons give for believing Freemasonry is not a religion is their claim that Freemasonry has no theology. But is this true? A definition of theology ("theos" = God + "legein" = to speak) is "to speak of God." Masonry speaks of God, demands belief in God, instructs each candidate how to worship God, informs each candidate that the true name of God has been lost, and then in a later degree reveals that lost name.

For example, Masonry clearly teaches theology during the Royal Arch degree (York Rite), when it tells each candidate that the lost name for God will now be revealed to them. The name that is given is Jahbulon. This is a composite term joining Jehovah with two pagan gods—the evil Canaanite deity Baal (Jeremiah 19:5; Judges 3:7; 10:6), and the Egyptian god Osiris (95:516; 58:226). This equating of God with false gods is something the God of the Bible strictly forbids (see Question16, point 2). "You shall have no other gods before me....You shall not worship them or serve them; for I, the Lord your God, am a jealous God…" (Exodus 20:3,5); "You shall not learn to imitate the detestable things of those nations" (Deuteronomy 18:9); "Who among the gods is like you, O Lord? Who is like you—majestic in holiness, awesome in glory, working wonders?" (Exodus 15:11 NIV).

The *Oxford American Dictionary* defines theology as "a system of religion" (107). Webster defines theology as "the study of God and the relations between God and the universe....A specific *form* or system…as expounded by a particular religion or denomination" (108). Masonry fulfills these definitions of theology. As we have seen, it has its own specific system and form of belief which clearly spells out exactly how the Masonic candidate is to perform his ceremonies before God. In the Lodge, this theological instruction is known as the Masonic Ritual.

As Joseph Fort Newton said, "Everything in Masonry has reference to God, implies God, speaks of God, points and leads to God. Not a degree, not a symbol, not an obligation, not a lecture, not a charge but finds its meaning and derives its beauty from God, the Great Architect, in whose temple all Masons are workmen" (18:58-59). Anyone who says the Masonic Lodge does not teach theology is uninformed or just plain lying.

10

Is the Ritual that is practiced in every Masonic Lodge really worship?

Another reason why Masons think Freemasonry should not be considered a religion is because Masonry "has no ritual of worship" as a church does, they say. But is this true?

Webster's Dictionary defines "worship" as "a prayer…or other rite showing reverence or devotion for a deity…"—for God (108). Do Masons have rites that instruct them how to show reverence and give devotion to God? The answer is "Yes." Masonry has 32 degrees of ritual instructing them how to live a good life before God and how to please Him. According to Webster, in actuality Masons are worshiping every time they practice the ceremonies of a Lodge. For example, Roberts admits:

> "Masons walk in His [God's] presence constantly….[In ritual the "lights"—candles] formed a triangle about the altar at which you knelt in reverence. They symbolized the presence of Deity….The Masonic altar can be said to be one of sacrifice….You have taken obligations [to God] that have sacrificed your self-interest forevermore" (79:57,64).

The *Standard Masonic Monitor* commands, "Let no man enter upon any great or important undertaking without first invoking the aid of Deity....The trust of a Mason is in God..." (54:17).

Finally, Claudy frankly confesses that "Freemasonry worships God":

> "Freemasonry's Lodges are erected to God....Symbolically, to 'erect to God' means to construct something in honor, in worship, in reverence to and for Him. Hardly is the initiate within the West Gate before he is impressed that *Freemasonry worships God...*" (55:23, emphasis added).

Here again the evidence clearly shows that Masons are practicing religion when they worship God in their Lodges. As Albert Pike admitted in *Morals and Dogma,* "Masonry *is* a [system of] worship..." (26:526, emphasis added).

11

Does the Masonic Lodge have religious symbols just like those found in a church or synagogue?

Another reason Masons give in claiming Freemasonry is not a religion is because it has no symbols that are religious like those symbols found in a church or a synagogue. But is this true? How can Masons say this when the building they meet in is called a "temple"? In the temple, which they believe is "sacred" (95:513), they offer "prayers" to a "deity." No man can join the Masonic Lodge unless he swears belief in Masonry's "Supreme Being." The deity they pray to is called "the Great Architect of the Universe." Masons must kneel at their "sacred altar" to make their "sacred vows." Masons swear to be obedient and do the bidding of their "Worshipful Master." In the Lodge the "Worshipful Master" has hanging over his head a symbol—a big letter "G," which they are specifically instructed signifies "deity."

On the Masonic "sacred altar" is placed a "Bible," a "Koran," or another holy book called the "Volume of Sacred Law." In the third degree, every Masonic candidate is taught to accept the Masonic doctrine of the immortality of his soul, and further taught that if he is found worthy enough while on earth, his good works will earn him a place in the "Celestial Lodge Above."

How can any Mason say their symbols are not religious? What else would anyone call the big "G," hanging over the head of the "Worshipful Master," other than a religious symbol? After all, Masonry instructs each candidate that the big "G" represents the sacred name of "deity." If Masons do not want to have religious symbols, why don't they change the name of their meeting place from a "temple" to a "building"? Why do Masons swear their secret oaths at the "sacred altar" rather than at a desk? After all, *Webster's Dictionary* defines "altar" as "a raised platform where sacrifices or offerings are made *to a god*…a table, stand, etc. used for sacred purposes in a place of worship…" (106).

If Masons do not practice religion and are not surrounded by religious symbols, what are they doing saying prayers in the Lodge? What about the funeral services the Lodge performs committing the departed Mason to the "Grand Lodge in the Sky"? Why are the secret oaths called "sacred vows"? Why call the leader of the Lodge "Worshipful Master"? Why is the Bible kissed? What is meant when the Bible, the Koran, or the Vedas are called the "Volume of Sacred Law" and placed on the altar in different Lodges in the world? Why talk about the immortality of the soul? The reason they do all of this is because Masonry is a religion and uses many religious symbols.

We have now seen that Masonry 1) does meet the definition of religion, 2) offers its own plan of salvation, 3) has its own religious creed, 4) has its own distinct confession of faith, 5) has its own specific theology, 6) has its own unique ritual of worship, and 7) uses symbols just like those found in a church or synagogue.

All of this clearly proves *Masonry is a religion*. The only thing Masonry doesn't do is allow its members to consider it a religion.

12

Should the Masonic Lodge be identified as a religion if it does not choose to identify itself as a religion?

Masonry claims it is not a religion. But because Masonry claims it is not a religion, does that change the fact that it *is* a religion? One example should be enough to show that claiming something is true when it is not is ridiculous.

Christian Science, via Mary Baker Eddy, teaches that when a man's heart stops beating and he dies, it is not really death, but only an illusion. Christian Science boldly claims there is no such thing as pain, evil, sickness, or death; there is only good. But calling pain and death an illusion (changing the labels) does not alter the feelings involved in these experiences. And if I experience the same feelings, what good does it do me to call these experiences something different?

The same is true of Freemasonry. The Lodge does not call itself a religion. But because certain people call Masonry a "fraternal organization" instead of a religion, this does not change what it is in experience. That's why two of Masonry's leading scholars, Henry Wilson Coil and Albert G. Mackey, have both concluded that Masonry is a religion.

Here is what is at stake. All Christians believe that there is only one true religion—biblical Christianity. Therefore, all other religions must be false. After all, the Bible declares, "Salvation is found in no one else [other than Jesus Christ], for there is no other name under heaven given to men by which we must be saved" (Acts 4:12 NIV). "For there is one God and one mediator between God and men, the man Christ

Jesus, who gave himself as a ransom for all men—the testimony given in its proper time" (1 Timothy 2:5,6 NIV).

If the words in these verses are true, and if Masonry is another religion—and according to Mackey and Coil it meets the requirements of Webster's primary definitions of religion—then Christianity is the true religion and Freemasonry must be considered another religion and therefore a *false* religion.

Some people attempt to avoid this conclusion by saying that Freemasonry is not a religion—it is just "religious." But it would be just as sensible to say that a man has no power but is powerful; or he has no courage, but is courageous; or he has no wealth, but is wealthy; or he has no patience, but is patient; or he has no intellect, but is intellectual; or that he has no honor, but is honorable.

Others say, "But the Lodge is not a church so it is not really a religion." As we saw earlier, Coil responds to this by saying, "If Freemasonry were not a religion, such as you find in a church, what would have to be done to make it so?" He says, "Nothing would be necessary, or at least nothing but to add more of the same" (95:512). Coil reminds Masons that, "The fact that Freemasonry is a mild religion does not mean that it is *no* religion" (95:512).

If anyone still doubts that Freemasonry is a religion, we can think of no one better to quote than Albert Mackey, who in *Mackey's Revised Encyclopedia of Freemasonry* writes:

> "We open and close our Lodges with prayer; we invoke the blessing of the Most High upon all our labors; we demand of our neophytes a profession of trusting belief in the existence and superintending care of God; and we teach them to bow with humility and reverence at his sacred name, while his holy law is widely opened upon our altars....*It is impossible* that a Freemason can be 'true and trusty' to his order unless he is a respecter of religion and an observer of religious principle" (96,II:847, emphasis added).

If you are a Christian involved in the Lodge, how can you in good conscience continue to practice false religion? As God's Word emphasizes:

> "For what do righteousness and wickedness have in common? Or what fellowship can light have with darkness? What harmony is there between Christ and Belial? What does a believer have in common with an unbeliever? What agreement is there between the temple of God and idols? For we are the temple of the living God. As God has said: 'I will live with them and walk among them, and I will be their God and they will be my people. Therefore come out from them and be separate,' says the Lord" (2 Corinthians 6:14-17 NIV).

13

Does Freemasonry conflict with other religions such as Christianity?

As we have noted in this book, though many Masonic authors state categorically that Freemasonry *is* a religion, they go on to claim that Masonry in no way conflicts with other religions. For example, Mackey in his *Encyclopedia* has written:

> "The *religion* of Freemasonry is not sectarian. It admits men of every creed within its hospitable bosom, rejecting none and approving none for his peculiar faith. It is not Judaism, though there is nothing in it to offend the Jew; it is not Christianity, but there is nothing in it repugnant to the faith of a Christian. Its religion is that general one of nature and primitive revelation handed down to us from some ancient and patriarchal priesthood—in which all men may agree and in which no men can differ" (96,II:847-48).

This statement reveals that Masonry does have a problem with biblical Christianity. The reason is because the Bible says, "And there is salvation in no one else [other than Jesus Christ]; for there is no other name under heaven that has been given among men, by which we must be saved" (Acts 4:12).

It is nonsense to say a Christian can hold to two different religious beliefs at the same time, especially when they conflict. The Masonic Lodge says it is acceptable for men to worship God outside of Christianity. Jesus disagrees. He said, "I am the way and the truth and the life. No one comes to the Father except through me" (John 14:6 NIV).

Jesus Christ teaches that He is the way to God—not Masonry, that He is the truth—not Masonic religion, and that spiritual life is found only in Him—not in Masonic doctrine and Ritual (John 14:6). In John 15:4,5 (NIV), Jesus teaches, "Remain in me, and I will remain in you. No branch can bear fruit by itself; it must remain in the vine. Neither can you bear fruit unless you remain in me. I am the vine; you are the branches. If a man remains in me and I in him, he will bear much fruit; apart from me you can do nothing."

If a person agrees with the teaching of the Masonic Lodge, he logically must deny Christ. A person is forced to choose between the Lodge and Jesus. He cannot hold both at the same time.

In conclusion, we have clearly documented that Masonic authorities themselves say Freemasonry *must* be considered a religion because it fits any standard dictionary definition of "religion." We've also seen that Freemasonry does teach, through its emblems, its working tools, and its Ritual, how a man may go to heaven—which means Masonry has its own plan of salvation. We have noted Masonry has a distinct creed, its own confession of faith, a definite theology, and a specific Ritual of worship. Its symbols are comparable to those symbols found in any church.

Henry Wilson Coil in his 15,000-word article proving Freemasonry *is* a religion correctly concludes: "Nothing herein is intended to be an argument that Freemasonry ought to be religion. Our purpose is simply to determine what it has become, and is" (95:513).

Freemasonry obviously *is* a religion. Whether you are a Christian, a Jew, or of another religious persuasion, if you are also a member of the Lodge, do you realize that you are actively participating in a conflicting religion? If so, then how can you also participate in the religion of Freemasonry?

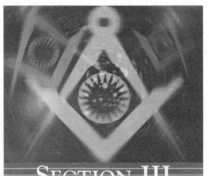

SECTION III

Where Does the Masonic Ritual Conflict with the Bible?

In the following seven questions we will examine the religious teachings of Masonry and compare them with the teachings of the Bible. Remember that it is the *Ritual* of Masonry that is the supreme authority (1:5). Individual Masons may disagree among themselves on various issues, but they may not disagree with the Ritual. And again, while there may be minor variations in the Ritual from state to state, these are largely insignificant. All Masonic Lodges accept the same basic interpretation of the Ritual that we will give.

During Masonic ceremonies various symbols are employed. Different symbols are used to identify the same idea or teaching—for example, both the compass and a sprig of acacia can symbolize immortality (79:62,80).

Masonic authorities universally acknowledge the importance of the Masonic symbols. Roberts admits, "Symbolism is the life-blood of the Craft....It is the principal vehicle by which the ritual teaches Masonic philosophy and moral lessons" (79:xi, cf. p. 11). Mackey confesses, "To study the symbolism of Masonry *is the only way* to investigate its philosophy" (90:5, emphasis added). In the questions below we will show how the symbols and rituals of Masonry teach things that are contrary to Jesus Christ and the Bible.

14

The Masonic Lodge teaches that all men, including Christians, live in spiritual darkness until they enter and become members of the Lodge. Is this biblical?

The Masonic Lodge teaches the nonbiblical view stated above in the first three degrees of the Blue Lodge, especially in the Entered Apprentice degree, where the candidate is told he will now be brought out of darkness and into the light. This teaching can also be seen from the fact that *light* is the first and most important symbol in Masonry (90:148,158). For the Mason, light symbolizes the seeking of truth. It is the goal of Masonic Ritual to bring the ignorant or unenlightened candidate to "Masonic Light" (79:21). Only Masonry brings light to the candidate, therefore only the Mason knows the truth (90:148,158). This means all non-Masons exist in spiritual darkness.

Proof that Masonry teaches this concept can be found by examining the Ritual of the first degree of Masonry. In the first degree, each candidate is instructed, "You have long been in darkness, and now seek to be brought to light." In the Ritual, when the candidate stands at the anteroom door, he knocks three times. On the other side of the door, the Junior Deacon also knocks three times and opens the door. He then says, "Who goes there?" The answer given by his conductor (the Senior Steward) is given in the Ritual itself:

> "Mr. [Peter Smith], who has long been in darkness, and now seeks to be brought to light, and to receive a part in the rights and benefits of this Worshipful Lodge, erected to God…" (58:29, cf. 13:4).

During our telecast, former Worshipful Master Jack Harris quoted Albert Mackey, who held the highest positions Masonry has to offer. Mackey was a thirty-third degree Mason and Secretary General of the Supreme Council of the Thirty-Third Degree Scottish Rite, a position he held for a great many years. In his book, *The Manual of the Lodge*, Mackey describes the candidate who seeks to enter the Masonic Lodge:

> "There he stands without [outside] our portals, on the threshold of his new Masonic life, in darkness, helplessness and ignorance. Having been wandering amid the errors and covered over with the pollutions of the outer and profane world, he comes inquiringly to our door, seeking the new birth, and asking a withdrawal of the veil which conceals divine truth from his uninitiated sight" (105:20, cf. 13:5).

But how can any Christian take the first degree of Masonry and say that he has "long been in darkness, and now seeks to be brought to light"? Is it really true that Christians are still in darkness and the only way they can enter the light is to join the Masonic Lodge? When you became a Christian, weren't you rescued out of darkness? Let's look at what the Bible says.

Jesus said, "I have come into the world as a light, *so that no one who believes in me should stay in darkness*" (John 12:46 NIV, emphasis added). He also said, "I am the light of the world. Whoever follows me will never walk in darkness, but will have the light of life" (John 8:12 NIV). Here Jesus teaches that *He* is the Light. He teaches that believing in *Him* removes spiritual darkness; He does not teach that any *ritual*, Masonic or other, removes darkness.

Colossians 1:12-14 (NIV) says, "Giving thanks to the Father, who has qualified you to share in the inheritance of the saints in the kingdom of light. For *he has rescued us from the dominion of darkness and brought us into the kingdom of the Son he loves*, in whom we have redemption, the forgiveness of sins" (emphasis added).

Another example is Ephesians 5:8, where the apostle Paul writes, "For you were *once darkness, but now you are light* in the Lord. Live as children of light (for the fruit of the light consists in all goodness, righteousness and truth) and find out what pleases the Lord. *Have nothing to do with the fruitless deeds of darkness, but rather expose them.* For it is shameful even to mention what the disobedient do in secret" (Ephesians 5:8-12 NIV, emphasis added).

Jesus and the Bible plainly teach that any person who believes in Him is no longer in darkness. If you are a Christian, how then could you enter the Masonic Lodge and swear that you are still in darkness and seeking light? In the first degree of Masonry, didn't you say that which is directly contrary to what your Lord and the Scriptures teach?

In Henry Wilson Coil's *Masonic Encyclopedia* he writes, "Light is everywhere the symbol of intelligence, information, knowledge, and truth and is opposed to darkness which symbolizes ignorance and evil. So, in the ceremonies, the candidate is said to be brought from darkness to light" (95:375).

But if Coil is right, then no Christian should take the vows of the Lodge, confessing that he does not have the truth and is living in spiritual ignorance and evil. The Scriptures clearly state that Christians "are *not* in darkness" and are "all sons of the light and sons of the day. We do not belong to the night or to the darkness" (1 Thessalonians 5:4,5 NIV, emphasis added).

How can a Christian participate in rituals and promote another religion that denies and opposes the teachings of Christ? Jesus Himself asks, "And why do you call Me, 'Lord, Lord,' and not do what I say?" (Luke 6:46).

15

Masons teach and believe in a universal Fatherhood of God and brotherhood of man. Is this biblical?

The Masonic Lodge teaches the nonbiblical view stated above in their first, second, and third degrees, but especially in the prayer of the Entered Apprentice and during their ceremony in the third degree concerning the legend of Hiram Abiff (79:84). Specifically, the Masonic Lodge teaches its belief in the unity and universality of all men as "one family" accepted by God regardless of race, religion, or creed (79:21). This Masonic teaching sounds good to most people. But if we examine it carefully, does the Bible really teach the concept of the universal Fatherhood of God and brotherhood of man, so that all men are automatically sons of God? Does the Bible teach that all men are in good standing before God even if they are ignoring God's Son?

The Bible does *not* teach any of the above, but Masonry *does*. During the ritual of the first three degrees, every Mason is introduced to the Masonic teaching concerning the Fatherhood of God. For example, in his discussion of the ritual encompassing the Masonic legend of Hiram Abiff, Allen E. Roberts in his *The Craft and Its Symbols: Opening the Door to Masonic Symbolism* instructs new candidates that "through these teachings the Mason will put into practice the brotherhood of man under the Fatherhood of God. In doing so, he will develop his character and personality in the image of the Great Architect of the Universe" (79:84).

Every man who has gone through the first degree of Freemasonry remembers the following prayer. It can be found in the *Standard Masonic Ritual and Monitor* of every state for the first degree (Entered Apprentice) of the Blue Lodge:

> "Vouchsafe Thine aid, *Almighty Father of the universe*, to this our present convention; and grant that this candidate for Masonry may dedicate and devote his life to thy service, and become a true and faithful brother among us! Endue him with a competency of thy divine wisdom, that, by the secrets of our art, he may be better enabled to display the beauties of brotherly love, relief, and truth, to the honor of thy holy name. Amen" (58:30, emphasis added, cf. 55:23; 54:17).

Masonic authority Carl Claudy admits that this prayer, at the start of the Masonic journey, forms the foundation of the Craft: "Among the most beautiful of Freemasonry's symbols, these express at the very beginning the fundamental principle of Freemasonry: the Fatherhood of God, and the Brotherhood of man" (55:24).

The Masonic temple itself is said to symbolize the idea of the harmony between the Fatherhood of God and brotherhood of man. For example, "The temple that the Craft is building is the unification and the harmonizing of the entire human family. This is summed up for us in the well-known lines: 'God hath made mankind one vast brotherhood, Himself their Master, and the world His Lodge'" (40:110). God Himself is said to be the ultimate "W.M. [Worshipful Master] working through His supervising Master Masons" (40:110).

But the Bible does not teach the universal Father-hood of God (that all Masons are in good standing with God and a part of His Lodge) and brotherhood of man (that all men can live in harmony even though they hold different religious beliefs). Scripture clearly teaches that sinful men only become children of God and attain favorable standing before Him when they place their faith in Jesus Christ as their Savior.

The following Scriptures prove that, apart from Christ, men may be the creation of God, but they are not the *spiritual* "sons" or "children" of God.

> "But *as many as received Him*, to them He gave the right to become children of God, even to those who believe in His name" (John 1:12, emphasis added).
>
> [Jesus said] "If I speak truth, why do you not believe Me? He who is of God hears the words of God; for this reason you do not hear them, *because you are not of God*" (John 8:46,47, emphasis added).

The apostle Paul describes the condition of all men before God prior to their faith in Christ:

> "And [you] were by nature *children of wrath*, even as the rest....Remember that you were at that time *separate from Christ*...and strangers to the covenants of promise, *having no hope* and *without God in the world*" (Ephesians 2:3,12, emphasis added).
>
> "[Men] being darkened in their understanding, *excluded from the life of God*, because of the ignorance that is in them, because of the hardness of their heart" (Ephesians 4:18, emphasis added).
>
> "But if anyone does not have the Spirit of Christ, *he does not belong to Him*" (Romans 8:9, emphasis added).
>
> "Whoever believes in the Son has eternal life, but whoever rejects the Son will not see life, *for God's wrath remains on him*" (John 3:36 NIV, emphasis added).

In Jesus' prayer to His Father, He describes the world's natural condition: "The world has *not* known Thee" (John 17:25, emphasis added). The Bible also teaches that someday Christ will return, "dealing out retribution to those *who do not know God*..." (2 Thessalonians 1:8, emphasis added).

When Masonry teaches that all men are already saved because of the Fatherhood of God and brotherhood of man, they are effectively inhibiting and preventing Masons from coming to a personal knowledge of Jesus Christ and having their sins forgiven. In this sense, Masonry is unbiblical (John 3:16).

In the above verses, notice first of all that if Jesus gives to those who believe on Him the right to become children of God, then all men were not children of God before that. This means that men are not *born* children of God, as Masonry teaches, and that God is not the Father of all men—spiritually or relationally.

Why? It seems Masonry has forgotten or ignores the account of man's Fall in Genesis—of Adam and Eve in the garden. The Bible teaches that man, through disobedience to God, sinned and broke his spiritual relationship with God. All men, although created by God, are not in a right relationship with God. Proof of this can be found in the Book of Acts where we read, "The God who made the world and all things in it…is Lord of heaven and earth….Being then the offspring of God…" (Acts 17:24,29). Notice that because God is the Creator, all men may be said to be His children, His offspring, in the sense of His *creating* them. But they are not His children *relationally or spiritually*. Here is the problem. Look at what God says to His children. God now "commands all people everywhere to repent" (Acts 17:30 NIV). Repentance means we must be willing to turn away from our beliefs and reliance on self and turn to and fully rely upon Christ's salvation provided for us.

How is it possible for a Christian to promote and defend a false teaching which says that all sinful men regardless of their relationship to Christ will go to heaven? The Scripture says a Christian should know better.

The Scriptures instruct Christians to proclaim that only through Christ will men receive forgiveness of their sins and be able to go to heaven. Jesus said: "I am the way, and the truth, and the life; no one comes to the Father, but through Me" (John 14:6).

16

Masonry teaches that the God of the Bible is the God of the Masonic Lodge. Is this true?

Masonry teaches at least three things about its God.

1. *The Masonic God is called the Great Architect of the Universe (G.A.O.T.U.) but must remain undefined.*

Coil's Masonic Encyclopedia states the following about God:

> "Men have to decide whether they want a God like the ancient Hebrew Jahweh, a partisan tribal god, with whom they can talk and argue and from whom they can hide if necessary, or a boundless, eternal, universal, undenominational, and international Divine Spirit, so vastly removed from the speck called man, that he cannot be known, named or approached. So soon as man begins to laud his God and endow him with the most perfect human attributes such as justice, mercy, beneficence, etc., the Divine Essence is depreciated and despoiled....The Masonic test is *a Supreme Being,* and any qualification added is an innovation and distortion....Monotheism...violates Masonic principles, for it requires belief in a specific kind of Supreme Deity" (95:516-17).

At one level, Masonry teaches that its God must remain undefined and unknowable. In keeping God undefined and unknowable, Masonry believes it can then "accept" all men's ideas of God. Masonry believes that by leaving God undefined, it can claim that it accepts the God of the Muslims, Hindus, Buddhists, Jews, Mormons, etc. What Masonry means is that its "boundless Divine Spirit" is really the one true God that all men worship.

But this is completely false and is actually dishonest. The God of Masonry does have certain characteristics—he is single (unitarian, not trinitarian), deistic (16:284; 103:4-5), the "Life Force of Nature" (16:281-351), and his secret name and true nature are described by reference to ancient evil and pagan gods and beliefs (16:137-355).

The simple fact is that the God or gods of Buddhism, Hinduism, Islam, Judaism, Christianity, Animism and all the other religions of the world are *not* the same God. To say that all gods are the same or that all religions teach the same fundamental truths is intellectual schizophrenia, *disrespect* for each and all religions, and *deception* to those to whom one teaches such falsehood.

Concepts of God throughout the world all conflict and disagree. For example, the God of Christianity, *Jehovah*, is infinite, personal, triune, loving, and holy. The deity of the Muslims, *Allah*, is unitarian (not triune); he is merciful, but he is not necessarily loving or holy. The deity of the Hindus, *Brahman*, is impersonal and monistic (neither unitarian nor triune) or polytheistic (a belief in thousands of finite gods, both good and evil). Buddhism is either polytheistic (believing *Buddha* is God and that there are hundreds of other good and evil gods) or completely *nontheistic*, claiming *there is no God*. Buddhism replaces God with a confusing state of being called *Nirvana*. Mormonism is different from all the above in that it is *henotheistic*—accepting belief in one central deity (*Elohim*) but accepting many lesser deities as well.

Masonry is wrong in teaching that all religions ultimately have the same concept of God. Masonry is also wrong in teaching that the God of all religions is the Masonic deity (16:288-302). The gods of the above religions are not the same. All the above religions teach that God is either personal, impersonal, holy, evil, unitarian, trinitarian, monistic, infinite, finite, loving, not loving, existent, nonexistent, etc.

So when Masonry claims that the God all men worship is the God of Masonry, this can't possibly be true. Masonry has a *distinct* concept of God that *disagrees* with almost all of these other religions' specific concepts of God.

If we compare the God of the Bible with the God taught in the Masonic Lodge, we are faced with irreconcilable differences. As Martin L. Wagner has correctly stated, "This Great Architect as conceived by Freemasons is not identical with the Jehovah of Christianity, but…is another and distinct entity" (16:321). He says they "are entirely separate and different, mutually exclusive and no syncretism can harmonize them" (16:300).

Masonic authority Albert Pike admits, "If our conceptions of God are those of the ignorant, narrow-minded, and vindictive Israelite…we feel that it is an affront and an indignity to him [God], to conceive of him as cruel, shortsighted, capricious, and unjust; as a jealous, an angry, and vindictive Being" (26:223).

Pike later referred to the ignorance and stupidity of most Christians and confessed: "The God of nineteen-twentieths of the Christian world is only Bel [Baal], Molach, Zeus, or at best Osiris, Mythras or Adonai, under another name, worshipped with the old pagan ceremonies and ritualistic formulas…" (26:295-96).

When Masons claim that the Lodge is "tolerant" of all faiths and accepts the God that all men worship, it is really engaging in dishonesty. The truth is that Masonry does not accept the God of any religion but changes each religion's belief in God into the strange, distinct Masonic view of God as the Great Architect of the Universe (G.A.O.T.U.) (16:288-302). Masonry falsely *claims* it is tolerant of other beliefs in order to attract men of different religious beliefs into becoming Masons. In actuality, a true Mason must forfeit his own religious beliefs in who God is and accept the new God of Masonry (16:288-302).

2. God's secret name is "Jahbulon."

The Masonic Lodge teaches in the Royal Arch degree that it knows the true name of God. The candidate is instructed that from now on the true name of God is Jahbulon.

The candidate is clearly instructed in his Masonic manual that the term "Jahbulon" is a composite term for Jehovah (Jah), Baal (Bul or Bel), and On (a possible reference to Osiris) (e.g. 58:226).

Masonic authorities such as Coil (95:516) and the *Masonic Ritual and Monitor* (58:226) admit that "Bul" or "Bel" refers to the Assyrian or Canaanite deity Baal and that "On" refers to the Egyptian deity Osiris. Wagner reveals the Masonic goal in this pagan trinity:

> "In this compound name an attempt is made to show by a co-ordination of divine names...the unity, identity and harmony of the Hebrew, Assyrian and Egyptian god-ideas, and the harmony of the Royal Arch religion with these ancient religions. This Masonic 'unity of God' is peculiar. It is the doctrine that the different names of gods as Brahma, Jehovah, Baal, Bel, Om, On, etc., all denote the generative principle, and that all religions are essentially the same in their ideas of the divine" (16:338-39).

But to equate Jehovah with the pagan god Baal—a god so evil that he led the Israelites into human sacrifice and other terrible vices—is blasphemous. Anyone who studies how evil Baal was in the Old Testament can see this clearly (cf. 31; 111-116). For example:

> "They forsook all the commands of the Lord their God...they worshiped Baal. They sacrificed their sons and daughters in the fire...and sold themselves to do evil in the eyes of the Lord, provoking him to anger" (2 Kings 17:16,17 NIV).
>
> "They built high places [altars] for Baal...to sacrifice their sons and daughters to Molech, though I never commanded, nor did it enter my mind, that they should do such a detestable thing..." (Jeremiah 32:35 NIV).
>
> "Among the prophets...I saw this repulsive thing: They prophesied by Baal and led my people Israel astray" (Jeremiah 23:13 NIV).

Baal was so evil a deity that to find the name of the one, true, holy God, Jehovah, linked with Baal and On in the rites of Masonry is blasphemous. God says, "Those who honor Me, I will honor" (1 Samuel 2:30). The apostle Paul writes, "To Him [God] be honor and eternal dominion" (1 Timothy 6:16). If you are a Christian, according to Scripture is it honoring to God to participate in a rite that maligns His divine name by combining it with the names of evil gods? Didn't God's severe judgment fall upon Israel because she combined worship of Jehovah with the worship of Baal and other pagan gods? Didn't God's judgment fall because of teachings like those found in Masonry? As former Past Master Mason Edmund Ronayne confesses: "The very religious philosophy and false worship which caused Jehovah to destroy His own temple, and banish into captivity His ancient people, are precisely the same philosophy and worship which modern Masons profess shall fit them for the glories of heaven" (68:126).

3. *Masonry teaches that its God is not the Christian God.*

Masonry teaches that God is one person only (unitarian) (51,V:51; 95:516-17; 16:321-51), while Christianity teaches that God is triune, not unitarian. An article by G.A. Kenderdeine, "The Idea of God in Masonry," cited in the Masonic magazine *The New Age* on pages 269ff. states, "Masonry holds and teaches that with all and above all there is God, *not* essentially a Christian Triune God" (19:37, emphasis added).

Masonry also teaches that God is an amalgamation of all gods: "[The Mason] may name Him [God] as he will, think of Him as he pleases; make Him impersonal law or personal and anthropomorphic; Freemasonry cares not....God, Great Architect of the universe, Grand Artificer, Grand Master of the Grand Lodge above, Jehovah, Allah, Buddha, Brahma, Vishnu, Shiva, or Great Geometer..." (60,II:110). But the Bible teaches that the Christian God alone is the one true God—He is not an amalgamation of all gods:

> "O Lord, the God of Israel, there is no god like Thee in heaven or on earth..." (2 Chronicles 6:14).
>
> "I am the Lord, that is My name; I will not give My glory to another" (Isaiah 42:8).
>
> "Acknowledge and take to heart this day that the Lord is God in heaven above and on the earth below. There is no other" (Deuteronomy 4:39 NIV).

Masonry also denies the biblical teaching on Jesus Christ.

Albert Pike taught that Masonry held that Jesus Christ was only a man and not God:

> "It reverences all the great reformers. It sees in Moses, the Lawgiver of the Jews, in Confucius and Zoroaster, in Jesus of Nazareth, and in the Arabian Iconoclast, Great Teachers of Morality, and Eminent Reformers, if no more…" (26:525).

Masonry claims that it does not offend a Christian's belief about Jesus Christ. For example: "We do not say to Christians that Christ was a mere man, whose life's story is only a revival of similar older [pagan] stories. To do any of these things would be irreverent. We utter no such words" (94:159). But Masonry *does* teach that Jesus Christ was merely a man (19:34; e.g. 20:126-27). The important Masonic Ritual called the Maundy Thursday Ritual of the chapter of Rose Croix states officially, "We meet this day to commemorate the death [of Jesus], not as inspired or divine, for this is not for us to decide" (20:127, cf. 91:75-77).

In his spiritual darkness or ignorance, an individual Christian Mason may choose to believe that Jesus was God and Savior of the world, but this is not Masonic truth. Those who consider themselves enlightened Masons hope that their unenlightened brethren will realize that all specific dogmas about Christ are in error. As Clausen emphasizes, it is important to "strip from all religions their orthodox tenets, legends, allegories and dogmas" (94:157). This is why the Masonic scholar Albert Pike asserts that Jesus was "a great teacher of morality"—but nothing more (26:525).

So it is neither fair nor true for Masons to say that Masonry does not offend Christians by teaching that Jesus was only a man. This is exactly what it teaches. Why does Masonry say that Christ was only a man and thereby offend the beliefs of Christians? It does this because it does not wish to offend the religious sensibilities of those Masons who are members of other faiths which deny that Jesus is the only incarnation of God and Savior of the world. For example, the unique nature and mission of Christ is denied by Hindus, Buddhists, Muslims, Jews, etc. In order to not offend these people, it offends Christians.

This is why nowhere in Masonic literature will you find Jesus called God or said to be the world's Savior who died for men's sin. To portray Him in such a light would "offend" men, and Masonry wishes to offend no one. The necessity for this approach can be found in the fundamental doctrines or Landmarks of Masonry (the Fatherhood of God, the brotherhood of man, and the immortality of the soul, Masonically interpreted). These doctrines *presume beforehand* that there is neither reason nor necessity that Jesus should be unique either as to His Person (God) or His mission (Savior). Thus, Masonry teaches that man already has a perfect standing with God. All men are guaranteed eternal life regardless of their personal religious beliefs. As a result, there is no need for God to incarnate (Philippians 2:1-8) in order to die for the world's sin (John 3:16) because the teachings of Masonry *assume* all men are saved or redeemed to begin with.

This is why Masonry completely excludes all particular biblical teachings about Christ such as His incarnation, redemptive mission, death, and resurrection. In fact, there is no biblical truth about Jesus Christ that is affirmed by Masonry as one of their Landmarks. This is why former Mason Edmond Ronayne confesses:

> "Freemasonry 'carefully excludes' the Lord Jesus Christ from the Lodge and chapter, repudiates his mediatorship, rejects his atonement, denies and disowns his gospel, frowns upon his religion and his church, ignores the Holy Spirit, and sets up for itself a spiritual empire, a religious theocracy, at the head of which it places the G.A.O.T.U.—the god of nature—and from which the one only living and true God is expelled by resolution..." (31:87).

The Bible clearly teaches that Jesus Christ is God:

> "In the beginning was the Word, and the Word was with God and the Word was God....And the Word became flesh, and dwelt among us..." (John 1:1,14).

> "Looking for the blessed hope and the appearing of the
> glory of our great God and Savior, Christ Jesus" (Titus
> 2:13).

Because Jesus Christ is God, He will one day judge
all the world, including all Masons and other men:

> "For not even the Father judges any one, but He has
> given all judgment to the Son, in order that all may
> honor the Son, even as they honor the Father. He who
> does not honor the Son does not honor the Father who
> sent Him" (John 5:22,23).
>
> "But when the Son of Man comes in His glory, and
> all the angels with Him, then He will sit on His glo-
> rious throne. And all the nations will be gathered
> before Him; and He will separate them from one
> another, as the shepherd separates the sheep from the
> goats....Then the King will say to those on His right,
> 'Come, you who are blessed of My Father, inherit the
> kingdom prepared for you from the foundation of the
> world.'...Then He will also say to those on His left,
> 'Depart from Me, accursed ones, into the eternal fire
> which has been prepared for the devil and his
> angels.'...And these will go away into eternal punish-
> ment, but the righteous into eternal life" (Matthew
> 25:31-34,41,46).
>
> "And there is salvation in no one else; for there is
> no other name under heaven that has been given
> among men, by which we must be saved" (Acts 4:12).

All of these teachings of Jesus in the Bible prove
that Masonry is wrong in its teaching about Jesus
Christ. How then can a Christian who claims to
believe in Jesus as his Savior continue to support the
false religion that denies his Lord? Did not Jesus
Himself say, "Why do you call Me, 'Lord, Lord,' and
not do what I say?" (Luke 6:46). Did not even Jesus
warn, "But whoever shall deny Me before men, I
will also deny him before My Father who is in
heaven" (Matthew 10:33)? And did He not say, "Not
every one who says to Me, 'Lord, Lord,' will enter the
kingdom of heaven; but he who does the will of My
Father who is in heaven" (Matthew 7:21)?

Masonic Ritual and oath demand that the Christian Mason's first allegiance is to Masonry, not to

Jesus Christ. Who then is the "Lord" of the Christian Mason?

In conclusion, Masonry is opposed to the Christian God. One of the leading Masonic scholars, Albert Pike, describes Freemasonry as follows: "Masonry, around whose altars the Christian, the Hebrew, the Moslem, the Brahmin, the followers of Confucius and Zoroaster can assemble as brethren and unite in prayer *to the one God who is above all the Baalim...*" (93:202, emphasis added). Notice that the term "Baalim" which refers to the false gods and idols that men worship (51,V:51-52) is also applied to the Christian religion. That means Christianity is considered to be as false a religion as all the rest.

Masonry only claims to be tolerant of the concepts of God found in other religions. In reality, it sees them as inferior to its own concept of God (51,V:47-52; 93:137,202). But then how is it possible for a Christian to support Masonry when it denies the true God, blasphemes Him, and leads people to worship a false God? Christians are exhorted to "live a life worthy of the Lord and...please him in every way...growing in the knowledge of God" (Colossians 1:10 NIV). They cannot do this by remaining members of the Masonic Lodge.

If Jesus came back today or you died and faced Him, how would you explain to Him why you continued to uphold the beliefs of an organization that rejects and denies Him?

17

The Masonic Lodge teaches that the Bible is only a symbol of the will of God and not to be literally obeyed. Is this true?

On the Masonic altar lie the square and compass and the Volume of Sacred Law. The Volume of Sacred Law is a *symbol* for the will of God.

Masonry has at least five distinct teachings about the Bible.

1. *The Bible is a piece of Lodge furniture*, a great "light" upon which the candidate obligates himself to Masonry (96,I:133; 51,I:132).

2. *The Bible is only a symbol of the will of God.* Masonry teaches that the actual contents of the Bible are *not* the Word of God. In *Coil's Masonic Encyclopedia* we read, "The prevailing Masonic opinion is that the Bible is only a symbol of Divine Will, Law, or Revelation, and not that its *contents* are Divine Law, inspired, or revealed. So far, no responsible authority has held that a Freemason must believe the Bible or any part of it" (95:520, emphasis added).

3. *The Bibles of other faiths are equally valid for the Mason.* Mackey's Revised Encyclopedia of Freemasonry states:

> "The Bible is used among Freemasons as a symbol of the will of God, however it may be expressed. Therefore, whatever to any people expresses that will [of God] may be used as a substitute for the Bible in a Masonic Lodge. Thus, in a Lodge consisting entirely of Jews, the Old Testament alone may be placed upon the altar, and Turkish Freemasons [Muslims] make use of the Koran. Whether it be the Gospels to the Christian, the Pentateuch to the Israelite, the Koran to the Mussulman, [sic; Muslim] or the Vedas to the Brahman, it everywhere Masonically conveys the same idea—that of the symbolism of the Divine Will revealed to man" (96,I:133).

4. *The Bible is only a part of the "revelation" of God.* In the Holman "Temple Illustrated Edition of the Holy Bible" Masonic leader Reverend Joseph Fort Newton wrote:

> "Thus, by the very honor which Masonry pays to the Bible, it teaches us to revere every book of faith…joining hands with the man of Islam as he takes oath on the Koran, and with the Hindu as he makes covenant with God upon the book that he loves best.…[Masonry] invites to its altar men of all faiths, knowing that, if they use different names for 'the nameless one of a hundred names' they are yet praying to the

one God and Father of all; knowing, also, that while they read different volumes, they are in fact reading the same vast Book of the Faith of Man as revealed in the struggle and sorrow of the race in its quest of God" (81:3-4).

In conclusion, virtually all Masonic authorities "establish three things: (1) that the Bible is only a symbol, (2) that a Mason is not required to believe its teachings, and (3) that some other book may be substituted for it" (51,I:132).

This is what Jesus and the apostles taught about the Bible:

> "He who rejects Me, and does not receive My sayings, has one who judges him; the word I spoke is what will judge him at the last day. For I did not speak on my own initiative, but the Father Himself who sent Me has given Me commandment what to say, and what to speak…" (John 12:48-50).
>
> "All Scripture is inspired by God and profitable for teaching, for reproof, for correction, for training in righteousness; that the man of God may be adequate, equipped for every good work" (2 Timothy 3:16,17).

How can a Christian Mason, who claims to believe that the Bible is the literal Word of God, help to promote an organization that denies the Bible is God's Word and denies Jesus' teachings on the Bible? Scripture tells us we are to live "worthy of the God who calls you into His own kingdom and glory" (1 Thessalonians 2:12).

18

The Masonic Lodge teaches that salvation and residence in the "Celestial Lodge Above" may be gained by Masons doing good works. Is this biblical?

By many different symbols Masonry teaches a doctrine of "works salvation"—that by personal merit and works of righteousness, the Masonic initiate will become worthy of salvation and eternal life. The candidate is told again and again that God will be gracious and reward those who build their character and do good deeds.

For example, the symbol of the "Sword Pointing to a Naked Heart" is said to "pointedly remind us that God will reward us according to what we do in this life" (79:76). In a similar fashion, the All-Seeing Eye, which symbolizes God, "pervades the inmost recesses of the human Heart, and will reward us according to our merits" (54:111, cf. 58:129).

The white apron or lambskin is "a symbol of Innocence, Purity, and Honor" (79:31). This is because, "The Lamb has in all ages been deemed an emblem of innocence. The lambskin is therefore to remind you of that purity of life and conduct which is *so essentially necessary* to your gaining admission to the Celestial Lodge above, where the Supreme Architect of the universe presides" (54:29, emphasis added). This same teaching is found in the *Holman Edition of the Holy Bible* that is published for Masons (81:4). Mackey states of the apron: "The pure, unspotted lambskin apron is, then, in Masonry, symbolic of that perfection of body and purity of mind which are essential qualifications in all who would participate in its sacred mysteries" (90:135).

The compass, the sprig of acacia, the scythe, and other symbols are all said to symbolize the immortality of the soul (79:62; 58:130-31). All of this is why Jack Harris concluded:

> "In all the rituals that I taught for eleven years, Masonry did teach how to get to heaven. They taught it with the apron that I wore, by my purity, life and conduct. They taught it in the Hiram Abiff legend of the third degree [symbolizing] the immortality of the soul. Through all their writings they say they are teaching the immortality of the soul to the Mason. But the Word of God tells me that the only way to have immortal life is through the Person of Jesus Christ. Never at any Masonic ritual did they point out that Jesus is the way of salvation" (13:35).

This is why Albert Pike says, "We must have faith in ourselves…" (26:30). And this is why the charge to the Master Mason at his raising states, "Let all the energies of our souls and the perfection of our minds be employed in attaining the approbation of the Grand Master on high, so that when we come to die…we gain the favor of a speedy entrance to the Grand Lodge on high, where the G.A. of T.U. forever presides, and where, seated at his right hand, he may be pleased to pronounce us upright men and Masons, fitly prepared [for heaven]" (54:125).

If you were to hear all of this in the Lodge, wouldn't you think that Freemasonry is clearly teaching that *you* can go to the "Celestial Lodge Above" if you live a pure and honest life? Isn't that "works" salvation? And if you're a Christian, when the Lodge teaches a man that by his good life and by his good deeds God will admit him into heaven, isn't that contrary to your Christian teaching?

In conclusion, there is absolutely no doubt that Masonry teaches that a Mason will inherit eternal life by his conduct and his personal merit. Masonry thus teaches a system of salvation by personal merit and good works. This concept of salvation is one which the Bible calls "another gospel." It is so contrary to God's way of salvation that Scripture places it under a divine curse (Galatians 1:6-8).

The following Scriptures give the biblical position on how a man gains eternal life:

> "To the man who does not work but trusts God who justifies the wicked, his faith is credited as righteousness" (Romans 4:5 NIV).
>
> "For by grace you have been saved through faith; and that not of yourselves, it is the gift of God; not as a result of works, that no one should boast" (Ephesians 2:8,9).
>
> "And this is the testimony: God has given us eternal life, and this life is in his Son. He who has the Son has life; he who does not have the Son of God does not have life" (1 John 5:11,12 NIV).

All of these verses in the Bible teach that salvation is a *gift* of God. Salvation comes solely by the grace [unmerited favor] of God, not by anything we can do to earn God's favor or by personal righteousness. By being a part of the Lodge, a Christian Mason is supporting "another gospel," a false system of salvation that lies to people about how they may be saved.

If you are a true believer in Jesus Christ, realizing this shouldn't you obey the biblical admonition in 2 Corinthians 6:17 (NIV): "Therefore come out from them and be separate, says the Lord"?

19

If a Mason has sworn allegiance to the Lodge, should he break his oaths?

God tells us to "have nothing to do with the fruitless deeds of darkness, but rather expose them. For it is shameful even to mention what the disobedient do in secret" (Ephesians 5:11,12 NIV).

But once a person is already a Mason, what should he do if he realizes that Masonry is wrong and sinful? What can someone do who has already taken the oath "for all time" (73:53)? Is that person bound to keep his oath? Here is what the Bible advises you to do:

> "If a person swears thoughtlessly with his lips to do evil or to do good, in whatever manner a man may speak thoughtlessly with an oath, and it is hidden from him, and then he comes to know it, he will be guilty in one of these. So it shall be when he becomes guilty in one of these, that he shall confess that in which he has sinned. He shall also bring his guilt offering to the Lord for his sin which he has committed....So the priest shall make atonement on his behalf for his sin which he has committed, and it shall be forgiven him" (Leviticus 5:4-6,10).

The Bible tells every person that if he swears an oath, if the implications are hidden from him, when he understands the implication and finds himself guilty of offending God's moral law, then he is guilty, and is to confess that he has sinned and to repent.

In the Old Testament a person was to go to the priest and confess that he had sinned and offer a sacrifice for atonement. Today, a Christian is to come to his High Priest, the Lord Jesus Christ, who has died on the cross for his sin; he is to acknowledge that he is guilty of swearing wrongly and repent of his oath, ask for forgiveness, and acknowledge that he will obey God in following the truth.

The Bible says, "If we confess our sins, he is faithful and just and will forgive us our sins and purify us from all unrighteousness" (1 John 1:9 NIV).

It is the duty of every Christian to break and renounce any evil oath that binds him to disobeying God. By taking the Masonic oaths, a person swears to uphold Masonry and all its teachings (whether he knows all of them or not). Swearing to uphold all that is included in the Masonic oaths is sinful, unscriptural, and should not be a part of the Christian's life for the following reasons:

1) They make a Christian man swear by God to doctrines which God has pronounced false and sinful. For example, Masonry teaches the false doctrine of "the Fatherhood of God," whereas Jesus taught that only to those who receive Him, who believe in His name, "He [gives] the right to become children of God" (John 1:12).

2) The Christian man swears to accept and promote the Masonic lie that Jesus is just one of many equally revered prophets in the world. He does this when agreeing that all religions can lead a man to God. But the Bible records Jesus' true words: "I am the way, and the truth, and the life. No one comes to the Father but through Me" (John 14:6).

3) The Christian swears that he is approaching the Lodge while in spiritual ignorance and moral darkness, when the Bible says Christians are children of light and are indwelt by the Light of the world. The Bible says, "For you were once darkness, but now you are light in the Lord" (Ephesians 5:8 NIV).

4) The Christian falsely swears that the God of the Bible is equally present in all religions. But the Bible says, "I am the first and I am the last, and there is no God besides Me" (Isaiah 44:6).

5) By swearing the Masonic oath, Christians are perpetuating a false gospel to other Lodge members who look only to the gospel of Masonry to get them to heaven. But the Bible says, "But even if we or an angel from heaven should preach a gospel other than the one we preached to you, let him be eternally condemned!" (Galatians 1:8 NIV).

The Scripture warns:

> "Do not be yoked together with unbelievers. For what do righteousness and wickedness have in common? Or what fellowship can light have with darkness? What harmony is there between Christ and Belial? What does a believer have in common with an unbeliever? What agreement is there between the temple of God and idols? For we are the temple of the living God. As God has said: 'I will live with them and walk with them, and I will be their God, and they will be my people. Therefore come out from them and be separate,' says the Lord. 'Touch no unclean thing, and I will receive you'" (2 Corinthians 6:14-17 NIV).

It is clearly the Christian's duty to break and renounce any evil oath that binds him in sin: "Have nothing to do with the fruitless deeds of darkness, but rather expose them" (Ephesians 5:11 NIV). Every Christian Lodge member should renounce his Masonic oath and confess it as a sin to his Lord. The Lord promises to forgive each one who will do so. ("If we confess our sins, He is faithful and just to forgive us our sins…"—1 John 1:9.) In this way the Christian will stop adding his influence to the sins of the Lodge whose false religion results in the damnation of so many souls (John 3:18,36; 8:24; 12:48, cf. 3:6-8).

Right now confess to God that you have ignorantly taken a vow against Him and His teachings and ask His forgiveness. Then notify your Lodge in writing that you have decided to leave the Lodge.

Tell them you believe that their teaching and their vows are not biblical, and as a Christian you can no longer participate according to 2 Corinthians 6:14-18 and Ephesians 5:8-17.

Conclusion

If you are a Mason or a Christian Mason, what should you do?

We have proven that Masonry is a religion. Masonry is a religion with specific teachings on specific topics which conflict with other religions. In particular, Masonry conflicts with Christian teaching.

A Mason who is not a Christian needs to ask himself the following: If Masonry *is* a religion, is it the *true* religion? Will it *truly* lead me to heaven? Does it *truly* honor and glorify God? Or has Masonry merely invented a new God and a new religion in order to defend the particular beliefs of Masonry?

In his encyclopedia, Coil confesses that *if* the idea that Masonry alone will get one to heaven is "a false hope," then Masonry should abandon that hope "and devote its attention to activities where it is sure of its ground and its authority" (95:512). But where *is* Masonry's authority?

Only the revealed Word of God, the Bible, can tell us the truth about God, about Jesus Christ, about ourselves, about salvation, and about life after death. Since Masonry denies God's Word on these subjects, how can it logically claim to be true? ("No lie is of the truth"—1 John 2:21.) But if Masonry is *not* true, how can you as a Mason continue to promote what is not true?

The bottom line for the Mason who is not a Christian is this: If Masonry is true, then he should follow Masonry and promote its teachings. But if Masonry rejects and opposes the truth—if it denies God and His Word, if it denies God's Son, if it denies God's plan of salvation, and if it offers men a false hope—then the Mason must leave Masonry and instead follow the truth of God.

Does the Mason who is not a Christian really desire to take the chance that he will discover that Masonry was not God's truth after it is too late? Or is he now willing to make an investigation of this matter (109)?

Jesus taught, "I am the way, and the truth and the life. No man comes to the Father but through Me" (John 14:6); and "This is eternal life: that they may know Thee, the only true God, and Jesus Christ whom Thou hast sent" (John 17:3). The Bible further teaches, "And there is salvation in no one else; for there is no other name under heaven that has been given among men, by which we must be saved" (Acts 4:12).

If you are convinced that you are a sinner, Jesus died and paid for your sins on the cross. If you are willing to confess your sins to Him and trust Him to make you a Christian, say this prayer:

> Lord Jesus, I know now that Masonry does not bring honor to You. I confess that I am a sinner. I believe that Christ died for my sins on the cross. I receive Him now as my Savior and ask Him to give me the resolve and strength to turn from what is evil and to live a life that is pleasing to Him.

If you prayed this prayer or have any questions on the Christian life, write us at the Ankerberg Theological Research Institute, PO Box 8977, Chattanooga, TN 37414, and we will send you material to help you grow as a Christian.

What of the Christian Mason? The Christian Mason also must decide. In this book and especially in our larger book on this topic, we have proven beyond any doubt whatsoever that Masonry is opposed to the one true God, it is opposed to the teachings of the Bible, it is opposed to the person and work of Jesus Christ, it is opposed to salvation by grace, and it is opposed to every major Christian doctrine. How then can a Christian possibly join in, live by, and promote the teachings of Masonry?

Jesus Himself warned, "Beware of the false prophets....Not every one who says to Me, 'Lord,

Lord,' will enter the kingdom of heaven; but he who does the will of My Father who is in heaven....Every one who hears these words of Mine, and does not act upon them, will be like a foolish man, who built his house upon the sand. And the rain descended, and the floods came, and the winds blew, and burst against that house; and it fell, and great was its fall" (Matthew 7:15,21,26,27).

Christian Masons must decide today whether they will remain Masons and deny their Lord, Jesus Christ, or whether they will do the will of their Father in heaven and leave Masonry. Centuries ago the prophet Elijah challenged the people of God who had forsaken the true God and fallen into the grievous sin of idolatry. He warned them, "How long will you hesitate between two opinions? If the Lord is God, follow Him; but if Baal, follow him" (1 Kings 18:21).

This question remains true for Christian Masons today. If the Lord is God, then follow *Him*. Do not maintain the hypocrisy of claiming to be a Christian while living your life in an organization that denies everything Christian. Either follow God or follow Masonry. Either live as a Christian or live as a Mason. Jesus Himself warned: "These people honor me with their lips, but their hearts are far from me" (Matthew 15:7,8 NIV).

If you are a Christian and right now you would be willing to leave the Lodge and obey your Lord, you may say this prayer:

> Dear Jesus, I confess that I have sinned against You in supporting the unchristian teachings of the Lodge. I now ask Your forgiveness and that You would give me the strength to live my life for You and to forsake the Lodge. Help me also to pray for and be a witness to my friends in the Lodge.

The decision you have just made is a hard one to make. Friends may not understand. You may be laughed at or threatened. If you are, remember this: You are in good company. Jesus said:

> "Blessed are those who are persecuted because of righteousness, for theirs is the kingdom of heaven. Blessed

are you when people insult you, persecute you and falsely say all kinds of evil against you because of me. Rejoice and be glad, because great is your reward in heaven, for in the same way they persecuted the prophets who were before you" (Matthew 5:10-12 NIV).

Finally, many pastors, elders, and deacons have no problem with accepting Masons as Christians and granting them positions of teaching and leadership in the local church. We urge such persons to reexamine this practice. Why? Because Masons are sworn to uphold the beliefs and practices of Masonry, which are contrary to Christianity (e.g., 92:74-75). How can such men be put in positions of leadership and authority when the Bible says, for example, "Deacons, likewise, are to be men worthy of respect, sincere....They must keep hold of the deep truths of the faith with a clear conscience. They must first be tested; and then if there is nothing against them, let them serve as deacons" (1 Timothy 3:8-10).

BIBLIOGRAPHY FOR REFERENCES CITED
(References with asterisks are recommended reading)

*1. Transcript, "Christianity and the Masonic Lodge: Are They Compatible?" (guests: William Mankin, Dr. Walter Martin), Chattanooga, TN, The John Ankerberg Evangelistic Association, 1985.

2. L. James Rongstad, *How to Respond to the Lodge*, St. Louis, Concordia, 1977.

3. The John Ankerberg Evangelistic Association, "Freemasonry on Its Own Terms," *News & Views*, Chattanooga, TN, The John Ankerberg Evangelistic Association, May 1986.

4. The John Ankerberg Evangelistic Association, "Is Freemasonry a Religion? and Other Important Questions About 'The Lodge,'" Chattanooga, TN, The John Ankerberg Evangelistic Association, 1986.

5. "The Bible and Freemasonry" in *Holy Bible—Masonic Edition*, Terminal House, Shepperton, London, A. Lewis (Masonic Publishers) Ltd., 1975.

6. "Freemasonry," *Encyclopedia Britannica Micropedia*, Vol. 4, p. 302.

7. Paul Tschackert, "Freemasons," *The New Schaff-Herzog Encyclopedia of Religious Knowledge*, Grand Rapids, MI, Baker, 1977, rpt., Vol. 4, p. 380.

8. E. L. Hawkins, "Freemasonry" in James Hastings (ed.), *Encyclopedia of Religion and Ethics*, New York, Charles Scribner's Sons, nd., Vol. 6, pp. 118-20.

9. The John Ankerberg Evangelistic Association, "Christianity and Freemasonry," *News & Views*, November 1987, Chattanooga, TN, The John Ankerberg Evangelistic Association.

10. E. M. Storms, *Should a Christian Be a Mason?*, Route 1, Lytle Road, Fletcher, NC, New Puritan Library, 1980.

*11. Committee on Secret Societies of the Ninth General Assembly of the Orthodox Presbyterian Church (meeting at Rochester, NY, June 2-5, 1942), *Christ or the Lodge?*, Philadelphia, PA, Great Commission Publications, nd.

*12. Stephen Knight, *The Brotherhood: The Explosive Exposé of the Secret World of the Freemasons*, London, Grenada Publishing, Ltd./Panther Books, 1983.

*13. Transcript, "The Masonic Lodge: What Goes on Behind Closed Doors?" (guests: Jack Harris, William Mankin, Dr. Walter Martin, Paul Pantzer), Chattanooga, TN, The John Ankerberg Evangelistic Association, 1986.

14. William H. Russell, *Masonic Facts for Masons*, Chicago, IL, Charles T. Powner Co., 1968.

*15. Shildes Johnson, *Is Masonry a Religion?*, Oakland, NJ, Institute for Contemporary Christianity, 1978.

*16. Martin L. Wagner, *Freemasonry: An Interpretation*, nd., np. (distributed by Missionary Service and Supply, Route 2, Columbiana, OH, 44408).

17. W. L. Wilmshurst, *The Meaning of Masonry*, New York, Bell Publishing Co., 1980.

18. Joseph Fort Newton, *The Religion of Masonry: An Interpretation*, Richmond, VA, Macoy Publishing and Masonic Supply Co., Inc., 1969.

*19. J. W. Acker, *Strange Altars: A Scriptural Appraisal of the Lodge*, St. Louis, MO, Concordia, 1959.

20. Jim Shaw and Tom McKenney, *The Deadly Deception: Freemasonry Exposed by One of Its Top Leaders*, Lafayette, LA, Huntington House, 1988.

21. Jack Harris, *Freemasonry: The Invisible Cult in Our Midst*, Chattanooga, TN, Global, 1983.

22. *Los Angeles Times* Wire Services, "Anglican Synod Condemns Freemasonry," *Los Angeles Times*, July 14, 1987.

23. W. J. McCormick, *Christ, the Christian, and Freemasonry*, Belfast, Ireland, Great Joy Publications, 1984 rev. (USA distributors: Issaquah, WA, Saints Alive in Jesus).

24. Kenneth W. Kemp, "What Christians Should Think About Creation Science," *Perspectives on Science and Christian Faith*, December 1988, pp. 223-27.

25. Arthur Edward Waite, *A New Encyclopedia of Freemasonry*, New York, Weather Vane Books, 1970 (combined edition).

26. Albert Pike, *Morals and Dogma of the Ancient and Accepted Scottish Rite of Freemasonry*, Charleston, SC, The Supreme Council of the 33rd Degree for the Southern Jurisdiction of the United States, 1906.

27. Isabel Cooper-Oakley, *Masonry and Medieval Mysticism: Traces of a Hidden Tradition*, Wheaton, IL, Theosophical Publishing House, 1977.

28. Corinne Heline, *Mystic Masonry and the Bible*, La Canada, CA, New Age Press, 1975.

*29. Alva J. McClain, *Freemasonry and Christianity*, Winona Lake, IN, BMH Books, 1977.

30. Edmond Ronayne, *Ronayne's Handbook of Freemasonry with Appendix (Mah-hah-bone)*, Chicago, IL, Ezra A. Cook, 1976.

31. Edmond Ronayne, *The Master's Carpet; or Masonry and Baal-Worship—Identical*, nd., np. (distributed by Missionary Service and Supply, Route 2, Columbiana, OH 44408).

32. Booklist for A. Lewis, Ltd. (Masonic Publishers), Terminal House, Middlesex, England, January 1979.

33. Osborne Sheppard (compiler and publisher), *Freemasonry in Canada with a Concise History of Old British Lodges, the Introduction of Freemasonry into the United States of America and Other Valuable and Instructive Information*, Hamilton, Ontario, Osborne Sheppard, 1915.

34. W. J. Morris, *Pocket Lexicon of Freemasonry*, Chicago, IL, Ezra A. Cook Publications, nd.

35. Manley P. Hall, *The Lost Keys of Freemasonry or the Secret of Hiram Abiff*, Richmond, VA, Macoy Publishing and Masonic Supply Co., Inc., 1976.

36. Henry Wilson Coil, *A Comprehensive View of Freemasonry*, Richmond, VA, Macoy Publishing and Masonic Supply Co., 1973.

37. Stephen R. Sywulka, "The Pope Uses Masonic Scandal to Stiffen Traditional Stance," *Christianity Today*, June 26, 1981.

38. F. De P. Castells, *The Genuine Secrets in Freemasonry Prior to A.D. 1717*, London, England, A. Lewis, 1971.

39. Edmond Ronayne, *Freemasonry at a Glance*, Chicago, IL, Ezra A. Cook Publications, 1904.

40. Foster Bailey, *The Spirit of Masonry*, Hampstead, London, Lucius Press, Ltd., 1972.

41. Harold Waldwin Percival, *Masonry and Its Symbols in the Light of "Thinking and Destiny,"* Forest Hills, NY, The Word Foundation, Inc., 1979.

42. Douglas Knoop, G. P. Jones, and Douglas Hamer (transcribers and editors), *The Early Masonic Catechisms*, London, England, Quatuor Coronati Lodge No. 2076, London, 1975.

43. George H. Steinmetz, *Freemasonry—Its Hidden Meaning*, Chicago, IL, Charles T. Powner Co., 1976.

44. *Masonic Square for 1975 and 1976* (bound volume), (Vol. 1, March 1975-December 1975; Vol. 2, March 1976-December 1976).

45. John Sheville and James Gould, *Guide to the Royal Arch Chapter: A Complete Monitor with Full Instructions in the Degrees of Mark Master, Past Master, Most Excellent Master and Royal Arch Together With the Order of High Priesthood*, Richmond, VA, Macoy Publishing and Masonic Supply Co., 1981.

46. John R. Rice, *Lodges Examined by the Bible*, Murfreesboro, TN, Sword of the Lord Publishers, 1943.

48. Kent Henderson, *Masonic World Guide*, Richmond, VA, Macoy Publishing and Masonic Supply Co., 1984.

49. H. V. B. Voorhis, *Facts for Freemasons: A Storehouse of Masonic Knowledge in Question and Answer Form*, Richmond, VA, Macoy Publishing and Masonic Supply, 1979 (rev.).

50. Rollin C. Blackmer, *The Lodge and the Craft*, Richmond, VA, Macoy Publishing and Masonic Supply, 1976.

51. Various authors, *Little Masonic Library* (5 volumes), Richmond, VA, Macoy Publishing and Masonic Supply, 1977.

52. The Ancient and Accepted Scottish Rite of Freemasonry, Southern Jurisdiction USA, *Ceremonies of Installation and Dedication*, 1954 (rev.).

53. The General Grand Chapter of Royal Arch Masons International, Committee on Revision of the Ritual, William F. Kuhn, et. al. (The Manual of Ritual for Royal Arch Masons), 45th Edition, 1983.

54. George Simmons and Robert Macoy, *Standard Masonic Monitor of the Degrees of Entered Apprentice, Fellow Craft and Master Mason*, Richmond, VA, Macoy Publishing and Masonic Supply, 1984.

55. Carl H. Claudy, *Foreign Countries: A Gateway to the Interpretation and Development of Certain Symbols of Freemasonry*, Richmond, VA, Macoy Publishing and Masonic Supply, 1971.

56. James Royal Case, *The Case Collection: Biographies of Masonic Notables*, The Missouri Lodge of Research, 1984.

57. Alphonse Cerza, *A Masonic Reader's Guide* (Thomas C. Warden, ed.), Transactions of the Missouri Lodge of Research, Vol. 34 (1978-1979), 1980.

58. Malcom C. Duncan, *Masonic Ritual and Monitor*, New York, David McKay Co., nd.

59. J. Blanchard, *Scottish Rite Masonry Illustrated (The Complete Ritual of the Ancient and Accepted Scottish Rite)* (two volumes), Chicago, IL, Charles T. Powner Co., 1979.

60. Carl H. Claudy, *Introduction to Freemasonry* (three volumes), Washington, D.C., The Temple Publishers, 1984.

61. Ezra A. Cook Publications, *Revised Knight Templarism Illustrated*, Chicago, IL, Ezra A. Cook, 1986.

62. The Free and Accepted Masons of Arkansas, Grand Lodge, *Masonic Monitor of the Degrees of Entered Apprentice, Fellow Craft and Master Mason*, Free and Accepted Masons of Arkansas, 7th ed., 1983.

63. Carl H. Claudy, *The Master's Book*, Washington, DC, The Temple Publishers, 1985.

64. Harris Bullock, et. al., *Masonic Manual of the Grand Lodge of Georgia, Free and Accepted Masons*, The Grand Lodge of Georgia, 1983.

65. Raymond Lee Allen, et. al., *Tennessee Craftsmen or Masonic Textbook*, Nashville, Tennessee Board of Custodians Members, 1963, 14th edition.

66. William W. Daniel, et. al., *Masonic Manual of the Grand Lodge of Georgia, Free and Accepted Masons*, Grand Lodge of Georgia, 9th edition, 1973.

67. Ezra A. Cook Publications, *Blue Lodge Enlight'ment [sic]: A Ritual of the Three Masonic Degrees*, Chicago, IL, Ezra A. Cook, 1964.

68. E. Ronayne, *Chapter Masonry*, Chicago, IL, Ezra A. Cook, 1984.

69. Grand Lodge of Texas, A. F. and A. M., *Monitor of the Lodge: Monitorial Instructions in the Three Degrees of Symbolic Masonry*, Grand Lodge of Texas, 1982.

70. Henry Wilson Coil, *Freemasonry Through Six Centuries* (two volumes), Richmond, VA, Macoy Publishing and Masonic Supply, 1967.

71. Awad Khoury (trans.), *The Origin of Masonry*, nd., np. (originally pub. 1897).

72. H. J. Rogers, *The Word of God vs. Masonry*, Van Alstyne, TX, B & R Publishers, nd.

*73. Alphonse Cerza, *Let There Be Light: A Study in Anti Masonry*, Silver Spring, MD, The Masonic Service Association, 1983.

74. H. L. Haywood, *The Newly-Made Mason: What He and Every Mason Should Know About Masonry*, Richmond, VA, Macoy Publishing and Masonic Supply, 1973.

75. Nobles of the Mystic Shrine, *Proceedings of the 90th Annual Session—Imperial Council of the Ancient Arabic Order of the Nobles of the Mystic Shrine for North America* (Iowa Corporation), New York, 1964.

76. Allen E. Roberts, *Key to Freemasonry's Growth*, Richmond, VA, Macoy Publishing and Masonic Supply, 1969.

77. Joseph Fort Newton, *The Builders: A Story and Study of Freemasonry*, Richmond, VA, Macoy Publishing and Masonic Supply, 1951.

78. John H. Van Gorden (ed.), *Masonic Charities*, Lexington, MA, The Supreme Council, 33rd Degree, Ancient Accepted Scottish Rite of Freemasonry; Northern Masonic Jurisdiction, USA, 1987.

79. Allen E. Roberts, *The Craft and Its Symbols: Opening the Door to Masonic Symbolism*, Richmond, VA, Macoy Publishing and Masonic Supply, 1974.

80. Henry C. Clausen, *Beyond the Ordinary: Toward a Better, Wiser and Happier World*, Washington, DC, The Supreme Council, 33rd Degree, Ancient and Accepted Scottish Rite of Freemasonry, 1983.

81. Holy Bible (Temple Illustrated Edition), Nashville, TN, A. J. Holman Co., 1968.

82. John Dove (compiler), *Virginia Textbook (containing "The Book of Constitutions," Illustrations of the Work, Forms and Ceremonies of the Grand Lodge of Virginia*, Grand Lodge of Virginia, nd.

83. Southern Jurisdiction of the United States of America, *Funeral Ceremony and Offices of a Lodge of Sorrow of the Ancient and Accepted Scottish Rite of Freemasonry*, Charleston, SC, 1946, rpt.

84. Southern Jurisdiction of the USA, *Ceremonies of Installation and Dedication...of the Ancient and Accepted Scottish Rite of Freemasonry*, The Ancient and Accepted Scottish Rite of Freemasonry, Southern Jurisdiction, USA, 1954.

85. Henry G. Meacham, *Our Stations and Places*, New York, Grand Lodge, F. and A. M. Committee on Lodge Sales, 1967.

86. Holy Bible—Masonic Edition, Philadelphia, PA, A. J. Holman, 1939.

87. Arthur Herrmann, *Designs Upon the Trestleboard: A Guidebook for Masters and Wardens*, Richmond, VA, Macoy Publishing and Masonic Supply, 1980.

88. William J. Hughan, et. al., *Freemasonry*, Washington, DC, Library of the Supreme Council, 33rd Degree, 1958 (rpt. from the *Encyclopedia Britannica*).

89. H. L. Haywood, *The Great Teachings of Masonry*, Richmond, VA, Macoy Publishing and Masonic Supply, 1971.

90. Albert G. Mackey, *The Symbolism of Freemasonry: Illustrating and Explaining Its Science and Philosophy, Its Legends, Myths, and Symbols*, Chicago, IL, Charles T. Powner Co., 1975.

91. Henry C. Clausen, *Practice and Procedure for the Scottish Rite*, Washington, DC, The Supreme Council, 33rd Degree, Ancient and Accepted Scottish Rite of Freemasonry, Mother Jurisdiction of the World, 1981.

92. Educational and Historical Commission of the Grand Lodge of Georgia, *Leaves from Georgia Masonry*, Educational and Historical Commission of the Grand Lodge of Georgia, 1947.

93. The Supreme Council, 33rd Degree of the Ancient and Accepted Scottish Rite of Freemasonry of the Southern Jurisdiction of the USA, *Liturgy of the Ancient and Accepted Scottish Rite of Freemasonry for the Southern Jurisdiction of the United States, Part Two*, Washington, DC, 1982.

94. Henry C. Clausen, *Clausen's Commentaries on Morals and Dogma*, The Supreme Council, 33rd Degree, Ancient and Accepted Scottish Rite of Freemasonry, Southern Jurisdiction of the USA, 1976.

95. Henry Wilson Coil, *Coil's Masonic Encyclopedia*, New York, Macoy Publishing and Masonic Supply, 1961.

96. Albert G. Mackey, *Mackey's Revised Encyclopedia of Freemasonry* (revised and enlarged by Robert I. Clegg—three volumes), Richmond, VA, Macoy Publishing and Masonic Supply, 1966.

97. William C. Irvine, *Heresies Exposed*, Neptune, NJ, Loizeaux Brothers, 1970.

98. "Freemasonry" in Richard Cavendish (ed.), *Man, Myth and Magic: An Illustrated Encyclopedia of the Supernatural*, New York, Marshall Cavendish Corporation, 1970.

99a. Legenda 32 (Part 1). (This is a Masonic source apparently used for instruction, circa 1920-1930. No publisher, author, or date is given.)

99b. Legenda, *Scottish Rite*, XIX to XXX, 26th degree (Part 2).

100. Henry Pirtle, *Kentucky Monitor: Complete Monitorial Ceremonies of the Blue Lodge*, Louisville, KY, Standard Printing Co., 1921.

101. Editorial by Francis G. Paul, The Sovereign Grand Commander, "The Test Never Changes," *The Northern Light: A Window for Freemasonry*, May 1988.

102. The Working Group established by the Standing Committee of the General Synod of the Church of England, *Freemasonry and Christianity: Are They Compatible?*, London, Church House Publishing, 1987.

103. The Baptist Union of Scotland (endorsed by the Baptist Union of Great Britain and Ireland), *Baptists and Freemasonry*, Baptist Church House, 1987.

104. Report of the Faith and Order Committee of the British Methodist Church, *Freemasonry and Methodism*, 1985 (presented to the General Assembly of the British Methodist Church and adopted by them Wednesday, July 3, 1985).

105. Albert G. Mackey, *The Manual of the Lodge*, New York, Clark Maynard, 1870.

106. *Webster's New World Dictionary*, Second Collegiate Edition, New York, Simon & Schuster, 1984.

107. *Oxford American Dictionary*, New York, Avon, 1982.

108. *Webster's New Twentieth Century Dictionary*, Second Edition Unabridged, Collins-World, 1978.

* 109. See C. S. Lewis, *Mere Christianity* (MacMillan); Henry M. Morris, *Many Infallible Proofs* (Master Books), and Os Guinness, *In Two Minds* (Inter-Varsity).

110. "Checking It Out" (Masonic Affiliates), *News & Views*, August 1986, Chattanooga, TN, The John Ankerberg Evangelistic Association.

111. A.E. Cundall, "Baal" in Merrill C. Tenney (ed.), *The Zondervan Pictorial Encyclopedia of the Bible*, Vol. 1, Grand Rapids, MI, Zondervan, 1975.

112. "Baal" in *Encyclopedia Britannica—Micropedia*, Vol. 1, Chicago, IL, University of Chicago, 1978.

113. "Baal" in *The New Schaff-Herzog Encyclopedia of Religious Knowledge*, Vol. 1, pp.390-93, Grand Rapids, MI, Baker, 1977.

114. Lewis Bayles Payton, "Baal, Beel, Bel" in James Hastings (ed.) *Encyclopedia of Religion and Ethics*, Vol. 2, New York, Charles Schribner's Sons, nd.

115. George A. Barton, "Baalzebub and Beelzaboul" in No.114, subsequent article.

116a. W. L. Liefeld, "Mystery Religions" in Merrill C. Tenney, *The Zondervan Pictorial Encyclopedia of the Bible*, Vol. 4, Grand Rapids, MI, Zondervan, 1977, cf.

116b. John Gray, "Baal—The Dying and Rising God" in Richard Cavendish (ed.), *Man, Myth and Magic: An Illustrated Encyclopedia of the Supernatural*, Vol. 2, New York, Marshall Cavendish Corp., 1970.

117. *Congressional Record*, Senate, September 9, 1987, pp. S11868-70.